It's a Jungle Out There!
Dealing with Difficult Behavior in the Workplace

Charles Mallory

American Media Publishing
4900 University Avenue
West Des Moines, Iowa 50266-6769 U.S.A.
800/262-2557

It's a Jungle Out There! Dealing with Difficult Behavior in the Workplace

Charles Mallory
Copyright © 1998 by American Media Incorporated

This publication is designed to provide accurate and authoritative information in regard to the subject matter covered. It is sold with the understanding that neither the author nor the publisher is engaged in rendering legal, accounting, or other professional service. If legal advice or other expert assistance is required, the services of a competent professional person should be sought.

Credits:

American Media Publishing:	Arthur Bauer
	Todd McDonald
Editor in Chief:	Karen Massetti Miller
Editor:	Jill J. Jensen
Designer:	Gayle O'Brien
Cover Design:	Polly Beaver

Published by American Media Inc.
4900 University Avenue
West Des Moines, IA 50266-6769 U.S.A.

Library of Congress Card Number 98-70376
Mallory, Charles
It's a Jungle Out There! Dealing with Difficult Behavior in the Workplace

Printed in the United States of America
ISBN 1-884926-81-9

Introduction

Each day, evolving business practices, technology, finance, and other factors influence and change the concept of work. A few short years ago, who could imagine large numbers of people able to work from home? cellular phones? faxing from your car? Science fiction then—reality now.

One aspect of work that technology and other factors won't change is that we interact with people during the course our work life. Short of having universal mind control, we'll always interact with different types of people. For the most part, this melting pot of influences and experiences makes for a greater mix of ideas in the workplace. But the downside can be the challenges we face when encountering those who have different psychological tendencies than our own. People with minor differences aren't such a problem. But if you're a shy, quiet type working with a verbal aggressor, interactions can be very stressful—for both parties.

Remember that each personality type has positive qualities. Every workplace needs people with drive to keep projects moving. We're all glad to have that detail-oriented person on our team when it comes time to check facts and assure ourselves that the numbers are correct. Our friendly coworkers can help create smooth-running customer relationships. When we're working at our best, each of us displays our most "functional" traits. But when we go overboard in any area, we can easily become "dysfunctional," creating problems for ourselves and our coworkers. But regardless of our differences, we can learn to work successfully with other people. It's simply a matter of knowledge. Information is power, and the more we know, the better we can function.

Using this guide is an important step toward dealing well with others in your current work situation. You'll also find the information in this book to be helpful when you think of moving to a new position and even in your personal life. When you apply these strategies, you won't feel as if you're chopping your way through the jungle. You'll enjoy walking a smoother path instead.

About the Author

Charles Mallory is the president of Mallory Marketing, a consulting firm that serves a variety of training and communication organizations in marketing and career counseling. He began researching and writing about interpersonal work dynamics in 1990 and is the author of the book *Workhealing: The Healing Process for You and Your Job* as well as the audiotape *Workhealing: Keeping Harmony Alive from 9 to 5*.

He has served both as a subordinate and supervisor—working with "wild animals" all the while. "I've learned some of my best lessons in these situations, although it was difficult at the time," says Mallory. "When I would tell friends that my workplace was a zoo, I really meant it."

Self-Assessment

Do you handle difficult people at work in the most productive, least aggravating ways possible? Completing this self-assessment will help you find out. Using the scale below, circle the number you feel applies to you in each situation.

4 = Always   3 = Usually   2 = Sometimes   1 = Rarely   0 = Never

1. I am able to work productively with difficult people. 0 1 2 3 4

2. My stress level stays acceptable when I work with difficult people. 0 1 2 3 4

3. I feel patient with difficult people. 0 1 2 3 4

4. Rather than try to work with them, I avoid dealing with difficult people. 0 1 2 3 4

5. I work productively with the know-everything, show-off type. 0 1 2 3 4

6. I work productively with the stalling idler type. 0 1 2 3 4

7. I work productively with the sniping type. 0 1 2 3 4

8. I work productively with the aggressive type. 0 1 2 3 4

9. I work productively with the super-sweet, overly agreeable type. 0 1 2 3 4

10. I work productively with the complaining, negative type. 0 1 2 3 4

Working your way through this book will greatly improve your skills in handling the workplace challenges that can arise from interpersonal differences.

● Table of Contents

Chapter *One*

People Aren't Bad—But Their Behavior Can Be

Chapter Objectives

▶ Distinguish between dealing with bad behavior and considering someone a bad person.

▶ Realize that your response, not another person's behavior, creates productive or unproductive outcomes for you.

▶ Realize that more alternatives exist for positive interaction than wishing the difficult person were different.

▶ Employ new ways of thinking that will help you respond effectively despite the difficult behavior of others.

Case Study

Think back to a time when you had a bad day. Perhaps the phone was ringing off the hook and when one call turned out to be a less-busy coworker asking for a minor detail, you snapped at her—why didn't she handle it herself? Maybe in traffic you screamed at a couple of drivers or even cut them off. Then when you got home, you might have yelled at your kids. Are you a bad person for this? No. You just had a bad day. What the bad day did was change your *behavior*. It didn't change your *worth as a person*.

Recognizing Bad Behavior

When coworkers behave in difficult ways, they're not bad people. They may just be having a bad day. But if you've held a job for even a short period of time, you've probably learned to recognize the difference between otherwise agreeable coworkers who have an occasional bad day and coworkers who display unproductive behavior nearly all the time. What's the matter with these almost-always unproductive people? Have they had enough bad days to warp their personalities? Who's to say? Some of your coworkers may have had lots of bad times and lots of bad treatment. As they moved through life, consciously or unconsciously, they developed various ways of interacting with people because of what they encountered and experienced.

1

> **When coworkers behave in difficult ways, they're not bad people.**

Although this book will highlight some of the most difficult behaviors that people display, keep in mind that *not all bad experiences = bad behavior.* No doubt you've met people who have been through harrowing personal experiences and yet are sweet and loving. Perhaps you've met others who have had everything handed to them but have sour dispositions and can think only of themselves. One key to our behavior is the way in which we use our personal traits and abilities as we respond to the experiences and the people we encounter. Following are three examples.

Example 1: Larry

■ Larry is the one person in the office from whom you don't dare borrow even so much as a paper clip. Sure it's company property, but for Larry, that paper clip is his. Office always neat, each of Larry's work items occupies a specific place. Didn't return the project file he loaned you? He'll pester you about it, even before the date you said you'd be done! Want him to move to a new office? That's a major emotional undertaking—and it'll take its toll on you too. Larry's also not a good team player because he's always concerned about his status. If he hears of someone else getting a better raise, a better promotion, or a larger office, Larry sulks.

A closer look at his life shows that, as a child, Larry was picked on by his older brothers, who often took his things—marbles, baseball cards, and rocks from his collection. In college, a roommate stole things from him. Now Larry keeps thinking, "Why am I a victim all the time?" Actually, Larry hasn't had more negative experiences than most of us; he's just more acutely aware of things being taken from him. As a result, he's highly territorial and possessive.

Example 2: Katherine

■ As the only child of a wealthy, well-traveled family, Katherine was surrounded by elderly relatives who lavished her with gifts and made her the center of attention. When she was young, the family servants responded immediately to her commands, and with no sibling competition, she quickly developed a sense of being able to move the world. Katherine's family name was influential in their city; later she moved away because she felt all her noteworthy accomplishments were overshadowed by the fact that she worked at her father's company.

Now, as a supervisor at a different company in a different city, Katherine's achievements are credited to her. No one here knows of the hometown stature of her family. However, as a boss, Katherine is soundly hated. She wants things done— now! She sees to it that her subordinates work as late as she does, whether they like it or not. They'd better not complain, either. As she constantly reminds them, they're lucky to have a job in today's business world. Katherine doesn't like the democratic workplace she sees the company becoming. In her department, she holds to the principle that what she says goes, just as when she was a child: The more she bossed, the more things happened. What Katherine doesn't realize is that her dictatorial behavior is counterproductive in today's workplace.

Example 3: Hal

■ Hal has a great mind, although he is very reserved and quiet. When he does speak up, his coworkers are amazed at his insights about company projects because he's ferreted out important details others often overlooked. Without being negative, a nay-sayer, or a "devil's advocate," Hal simply assesses information from all sides and saves his organization from many potential problems. If not for his shyness, Hal would go far in his company. But because the CEO is forceful and loud, Hal barely speaks in his presence, although Hal is just as smart or smarter than his boss. Hal's subordinates, secretary, and assistant have learned they can break rules without reprimands. When peers come to him for a decision, Hal equivocates, not really wanting to tell them what to do.

As a child, Hal's parents didn't want to listen to him and said, "Children should be seen and not heard." At school, he was smaller than the other kids, who always picked on him. He learned it was safer not to speak up in class, and by his college years, shyness overwhelmed him. As an adult, Hal has shed some of his shyness, but he still limits his own greatness.

Identifying Positive Qualities

Larry, Katherine, and Hal share traits with you and your coworkers. They are "marble cake" characters, comprised of light and dark elements, good and bad qualities. What confounds you is what you consider to be their bad behavior. Remember, coworkers don't act up simply to inconvenience you (at least not most of the time; there may be sadistic types who would try that!). They simply deal with people in the ways that have been successful for them in the past. You do the same yourself!

Take a Moment

Think about difficult behaviors others display that seem to be "ruining" your life. Remember the statement about "marble cake" people, and review your experiences with three (or more) challenging people at work. Put aside negative aspects, and identify three assets for each person. You'll be better able to put negative behavior in perspective when you also remember positive characteristics.

Person's Name	Assets
1. _____	a. _____
	b. _____
	c. _____
2. _____	a. _____
	b. _____
	c. _____
3. _____	a. _____
	b. _____
	c. _____

1

11

Fortunately, you don't have to complete a Ph.D. in psychology to figure out your coworkers' motives. Even so, you can learn how to work with such people in productive ways that create the least amount of stress for everyone. The idea is not to change *them,* because you cannot change another person's behavior. Changing *your own* reactive behaviors and responses, however, helps smooth out the path you walk at work each day.

Controlling Your Response

Altering the way you respond reduces others' incentive for behaving in difficult ways. For example, if your supervisor barks rudely all day, and you scamper around trying to get everything done, you only reinforce the type of behavior that helps him or her feel comfortable. If you respond in a different way, one that reduces the opportunity for displays of bad behavior, your experience of your supervisor will be less difficult now and in the future. Using our previous examples, consider how each person's bad behavior produced the desired result.

> **Altering the way you respond reduces others' incentive for behaving in difficult ways.**

Person	Behavior	Result
Larry	Territorial	People leave "his property" alone; he feels secure.
Katherine	Demanding	People get the work done; she feels secure.
Hal	Shy	Avoids challenges by others; he feels secure.

When you consider ways to handle difficulties, keep in mind that your goal is not to circumvent others' behavior in an attempt to *force* them into a different mode. If you think, "Okay, I've always responded mildly to my boss. Now I'm really going to let him have it with both barrels! That'll make him change," you're likely to be disappointed. The *opposite* of any action does not guarantee the right reaction.

Choosing to bulldoze your way with strong-willed bosses whom you've meekly obeyed in the past probably won't work. If, as a supervisor, you've ignored timid workers and now decide to instantly pull them out of their shells, your chances for success are small. If coworkers are lazy and you've been demanding in the past, adopting a *who cares* attitude won't change a thing for the better. The idea is to respond in ways that are more beneficial to your own well-being.

By appreciating why particular types of people behave in certain ways, you can more easily recognize a variety of alternatives for responding to behaviors that are difficult for you to handle. Remember that nothing is completely black or white. If someone behaves one way, and you've been less than successful in dealing with that person, the information and exercises in this book can help you learn to respond differently and get better results. You'll need to become aware of verbal communication, body language, and day-to-day interactions, as well as the ergonomics of your office spaces and meeting setups, how reports or team work are assigned, the requirements for project completion, and so forth.

> **By appreciating why particular types of people behave in certain ways, you can more easily recognize a variety of alternatives for responding to behaviors that are difficult for you to handle.**

For each type of difficult behavior examined in the following chapters, you'll find an array of possible reasons why people act this way and a list of strategies. You can employ these responses to help you deal with difficult behaviors. Like learning to ride a bike, it's easier than it sounds. Although you might have dreaded the whole learning process, once you knew how to pedal, use the brakes, and steer, you were on your way. In dealing with difficult behaviors, you don't have to build yourself a bike—you just have to become more aware of how to ride it.

Developing Alternatives for Positive Interaction

Dealing with the difficult behavior of coworkers and superiors takes time and energy. Use your energy productively by refusing to wallow in emotional thinking.

◆ **Stop wishing the person were different.**
Have you met anyone who can honestly claim, "I really changed that person"? No one can "change" another person. People don't change unless and until they are ready—for their own reasons. Replace your wishful thinking with awareness that new responses will help you be better able to handle challenging people.

◆ **Consider your experiences with difficult behavior as valuable career-building education.**
While your local college community bulletin won't list a course specifically tailored to help you get along with time-wasting coworkers or inept bosses, each day you productively respond to difficult behavior, you're learning useful skills that apply throughout your career and your life.

Eliminating Ineffective Thinking

Below are three dangerous mind-sets that can sabotage your responses to difficult behavior. You may know of others. Learn to recognize narrow thinking, and make an effort to eliminate it from your life. Use "out-of-the-box" thinking, and you'll be amazed at how many creative solutions appear.

Learn to recognize narrow thinking, and make an effort to eliminate it from your life.

◆ **Either/Or thinking (sometimes it's either/or/or)**
Whatever the situation, either/or thinking implies that only one or two outcomes may occur. If it's not A, then it's B, or maybe C. As with the wealth of choices that exist in a supermarket or shopping mall, more than one or two options are available for any situation. Today, you might choose to eat chocolate-covered almonds, but tomorrow, you may prefer carrots instead. Be open to a variety of possibilities.

◆ **Victory vs. Defeat thinking**
"If I win, someone loses," says this old style of thinking. If for some reason, your supervisor changed from a demanding person to a cowering wimp, would you really be the victor? Without forcefulness, your boss might not be able to explain to the CEO why you deserve a big raise. Victory is not the opposite of defeat. Many acceptable alternatives fall within this range.

◆ **Progress as a Direct Path thinking**
If you think progress can be charted in a straight, upward-moving line, think again. Most often, success reveals itself as a zigzag path. Some days, you do well. Some days present setbacks. Every day won't hold a delightful new upswing as you work toward your goals. But if the general direction of your path moves forward, you'll be making progress. As the saying goes, "Some days, you're a bug; some days, you're the windshield."

Take a Moment

Think about whether you've employed thinking that can sabotage your responses to others. Write down a statement or thought that falls into each of these patterns.

Either/Or thinking
Your statement(s): _____

_____

Victory vs. Defeat thinking
Your statement(s): _____

_____

Progress as a Direct Path thinking
Your statement(s): _____

_____

Compare your statements in the exercise above to those in the examples below. By appreciating that all people can occasionally exhibit bad behavior, you can begin to recognize more productive ways of responding to difficult situations.

Either/Or Thinking

When you find yourself thinking:	*Think instead:*
If I don't solve this, I'll go crazy!	One way or another, I'll cope with this.
This person will never change.	Time changes everything, and I can deal with this in my own way. I don't have to change this person.
My supervisor will never understand!	I will do my best and handle things.
I'll never be happy here until I get a new boss (or coworker).	I will make my life work.

Victory vs. Defeat Thinking

When you find yourself thinking:	*Think instead:*
If she keeps showing off, I'll never get ahead here.	It's her day to shine. I'll have my turn at another time.
This is the third time I didn't get a raise. They're never going to give me one!	I'm not happy with this. I need to talk with my manager about what's expected of me and my work.
He is the boss's pet. The rest of us don't have a chance.	It's my job to do the best I can do. This isn't a race. I only need to do as well as I possibly can.

Progress as a Direct Path Thinking

When you find yourself thinking:	*Think instead:*
I'll never get ahead here.	This is just a "down" time. I'll keep working for better opportunities.
It doesn't matter what I do. She won't change.	I'm going to deal with her in the most intelligent way I can, and that's it. I'll conserve the rest of my energy for other things.
I'm putting a lot of effort into making this work and getting nothing for it.	Sometimes, progress isn't evident right away, but it shows up later. I'll be patient.

Thinking and Responding Productively

When faced with a difficult workplace situation, you may instinctively feel that you've encountered a bad person. But considering someone a *bad person* is not as productive as recognizing that you're simply dealing with a case of *bad behavior.* Once you can recognize that *your response,* not another person's behavior, creates productive or unproductive outcomes for you, many alternatives for positive interaction appear. By employing new ways of thinking, you can respond effectively despite the difficult behavior of others.

In the following chapters, you'll encounter several personality types described in terms of their animal counterparts. As you read the descriptions, you'll be able to see more clearly that each personality type and each person has positive and negative characteristics. Only when negative behaviors in the workplace outweigh the positive do they become problems. Only then does the behavior become difficult, requiring us to respond in different ways and help keep our workplaces productive.

Self-Check: Chapter One Review

Answers to the following questions appear on page 97.

1. True or False?
   Everyone who has bad experiences will exhibit bad behavior.

2. True or False?
   The problem is not difficult people; the problem is bad behavior.

3. True or False?
   The most productive way to deal with difficult behavior is to change your response and encourage a different result.

4. What three ways of thinking can sabotage your efforts?

   a. _____

   b. _____

   c. _____

Chapter *Two*

Peacocks: They Love to Show Off

Chapter Objectives

▶ Appreciate the motivation behind a know-it-all type.

▶ Distinguish between two types of Peacocks.

▶ Determine which strategies work best with Peacocks.

Case Study

Rudy walked into the office the Monday after a three-day weekend. Phones were ringing off the hook, the project-launch was scheduled to start in 20 minutes, and his in-box had mushroomed to twice its normal size.

James didn't seem concerned though. He cruised from office to office, looking for eye contact from anyone so he could chat about his weekend at the lake. To the guys, he boasted about his daredevil stunts—like swamping a canoe in the wake of his high-horsepower engine. To the women, he bragged about his water-skiing prowess and the cheers from the tanning crowd on the beach.

Rudy wasn't going to fall for it. When James stuck his head in Rudy's office and asked, "Hey, how was your weekend?" he curtly replied, "Okay, but I'm busy right now." Rudy didn't want to be rude, but he needed to deflect James, or he wouldn't get anything done.

What's Going On Here?

Do you know someone like James? To hear him talk about any event in his life, you'd think he won the Nobel prize. He won't shut up in meetings, whether he's contributing or not. Mention a household project, a car repair you're making, or even a family squabble, and James quickly tells you what's wrong and how to do it right. People like James can be difficult to work with, as Rudy discovered.

■ Although Rudy's project-launch meeting didn't include James, Rudy needed his help with part of the work. After the meeting, Rudy stopped at his office to give him his assignment, carefully explaining what James needed to do, but James barely paid attention. "I hope you're listening carefully to these directions," Rudy warned. "We're on a tight deadline, an important client is involved, and there's no margin for error."

Case Study

2

"Error?" James said, laughing. "When have I made a mistake that hurt this company?" Rudy could name five, but he decided to keep his mouth shut.

During the next two weeks, Rudy checked with James a couple of times, and James reassured Rudy that he was on schedule. "I'll produce," he promised. "Just leave me alone so I can."

A month passed, and James handed in his work. Rudy saw that his concerns were justified—James' results were weak, reflecting his lackluster efforts. Rudy commented on the poor quality.

"This is as good as you'll get!" James fired back. "The information just isn't there. It's really a start-from-scratch sort of project." Although James had many other excuses, Rudy knew that better results were possible. Now Rudy had to take up the slack. By the end of the day Friday, Rudy had figured out which parts of the project he'd work on at home and which parts he'd have to do in the office over the weekend.

As he planned, Rudy could hear James bragging to the others about his upcoming weekend activities. Sounded like it was back to the boat for James. Rudy could feel a headache coming on. He gritted his teeth and secretly wished James would have a serious accident.

Recognizing Peacock Behavior

Peacocks are perhaps the most challenging workplace animals to handle. They can be both incompetent and forceful, a difficult combination. The foundation for Peacock behavior, believe it or not, is low self-esteem. They might act bold and confident, but most of it is just an act. People who are truly accomplished don't need to act a certain way to prove themselves. Instead, they know their performance and achievements demonstrate their skills.

> **Peacocks can be both incompetent and forceful, a difficult combination.**

Workplace Peacocks appear in two major categories:

1. People who have had some truly outstanding or recent high-level accomplishment and temporarily get a swelled head. This type is rare because Peacock behavior doesn't usually appear when people feel truly secure about themselves.

2. People who regularly inflate minor accomplishments to boost their own egos.

The most common types of workplace Peacocks don't have true accomplishments in their backgrounds.

The most common types of workplace Peacocks don't have true accomplishments in their backgrounds. Instead, they build their egos by exaggerating small accomplishments or semisuccesses. Because they crave attention, these Peacocks appear as know-it-alls who feel the rest of the world *must* benefit from hearing everything they have to say.

Take a Moment

Can you recognize peacock behavior? On the lines below, indicate which of the types of peacock behavior described above are being demonstrated by writing 1 or 2 in the answer blank. Suggested answers are on page 97.

____1. Won an industry-wide award and was so suprised he or she bragged about it for a month.

____2. Is acquainted with well-known people and regularly drops names to let others know it.

____3. Informs other team members whenever he or she has met a deadline or achieved a goal, no matter how trivial.

Like all other workplace animals, Peacocks display both good and bad qualities. In their favor, Peacocks' strong personalities, persuasive abilities, and ability to promote themselves can take them into good, well-paying positions that bring some degree of respect. And because their feelings are not easily hurt, they often face mountains of criticism with a can-do attitude that helps the company and everyone in it succeed. However, Peacock characteristics can go astray when Peacocks talk too much, offer unwanted advice, interrupt frequently, and take over when it's not their place. Peacocks' strong personalities can take them places in life, even without substance for support, but their bluster doesn't work forever.

2

Case Study: Lisa and the Peacock Corinne

■ When Corinne started work at the architectural firm, all anyone could talk about was her prestigious college award and amazing ideas. But her coworker Lisa soon discovered that Corinne was not an ideal coworker.

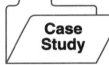

Case Study

Corinne managed to look important and act busy. But the office secretary, an aspiring architect herself, was actually handling things that were Corinne's responsibility, duties that shouldn't have been delegated. Corinne was also able to put herself in the position of being assigned to plum projects. When a less-desirable project came up, she acted so busy that the work fell to Lisa. But Lisa knew the truth: she worked harder and better, with good results.

Lisa thought the bubble would burst someday, but it didn't. Frustrated, Lisa told her supervisor about the situation. The supervisor, new and relatively untrained, decided to fire the secretary and reprimand Corinne. Corinne ended up hating Lisa, and because many coworkers sided with Corinne, Lisa found herself with fewer friends. Her boss didn't admire Lisa for telling the truth because it caused him a lot of grief. The icing on the rotten cake for Lisa was that Corinne was still assigned to better projects because the managers all seemed to think she was more professional and in control. After all, she hadn't resorted to tattling on a coworker!

Take a Moment

How could Lisa have handled this difficult situation more effectively? Write your answer in the space below.

_____

_____

_____

_____

Dealing Successfully with Peacocks

Don't let frustration get the best of you when dealing with workplace Peacocks. Follow these eight strategies for success with Peacock behavior:

Strategy 1: Let Peacocks believe they're Number One.

You don't need to prove that Peacocks aren't as good as they think they are.

Just as you don't need to waste time puffing up egos, you don't need to prove that Peacocks aren't as good as they think they are. You won't gain any advantage from trying to cut them down to size or show them they're not so big.

Remember, you can't teach the Peacock anything. Your negative effort will only build a higher wall between you. You say a wall is okay? Keep in mind that with their strong personalities, Peacocks often have great influence over others, whether or not that influence is warranted. Remember, too, that you must work with Peacocks. Trying to teach them hard lessons will not help you in the long run if you have to work on team projects or if you have to delegate or report to them.

Letting Peacocks think they're Number One means that you *don't bother trying to disprove their attitude.* Even if Peacocks manage to be the top producers, the most popular managers, or get the biggest raises, life will take care of the role they eventually occupy.

Strategy 2: Listen more than you would to others. Peacock egos need it.

Listening to Peacocks *will* take some extra time. Talking to others (which may also include bragging) helps them feel better and provides input they need to function. Listening a bit more does not give Peacocks license to interrupt you constantly, talk whenever they want, and occupy all of your time. You don't need to act deeply interested or listen endlessly; you only need to offer somewhat more communication time than you might with more independent workers.

Accommodate Peacocks, but only to a point. If time really gets to be a problem, offer alternatives such as, "That sounds interesting, but I'm really busy right now. Let's talk later." Don't let frustration with Peacocks overwhelm you. Remind yourself that your personal style is just different and may be nearly the opposite of what Peacocks display, especially if you're more independent and need little socializing in the course of your workday.

Strategy 3: Try not to challenge Peacocks in front of others.

One of the worst things you can do is challenge Peacocks in the presence of others. That's what Darius found out in a meeting when he got tired of Jeff's forceful assertions. "Jeff, you continue to try to persuade us to follow your line of thinking on this project, but what about the research?" Darius asked. "Do you have any statistics to back up your assertions? On our last project, you wanted us to go with that method. We tried it and failed, so why do you think we should listen to you this time?"

Bad move! Peacock Jeff likely heard several messages he can't appreciate:

♦ "You didn't do your homework."

♦ "You're trying to persuade us based on your personality alone" (with its hidden message ". . . and your personality isn't enough to convince us.")

♦ "Your previous idea failed."

2

> You don't need to act deeply interested or listen endlessly; you only need to offer some- what more communication time than you might with more indepen- dent workers.

25

That these three messages are true is not as critical as the fact that this Peacock was presented with the information in front of others.

Peacocks don't expect others to defy them at all, let alone with facts!

Because Peacocks have low self-esteem, they often exaggerate their achievements and dramatize stories they tell. They need to appear larger than life, to themselves and to others. Even if it doesn't seem fair to you, Peacocks don't expect others to defy them at all, let alone with facts! While it's right to use facts (see Strategy 6), just don't present them to Peacocks in front of others if you can avoid it. If you must handle Peacocks in a group setting, use other strategies from this chapter to do so. And take special care not to ridicule or embarrass them in the process.

Strategy 4: Acknowledge what Peacocks do well and use their skills when delegating.

When dealing with Peacocks, you might think it best to avoid saying things like, "You were certainly right on that Widget project," or "It's amazing what you sold last month," because you think you'll only inflate an already puffed-up sense of self-worth. But because Peacocks lack self-esteem, they need others to acknowledge their accomplishments. You won't be modestly thanked, as you would by a non-Peacock. Instead, you're likely to hear of the success until you're sick of it. But it's possible that with enough honest confirmation of achievements, Peacocks won't feel as much need to promote themselves.

It's possible that with enough honest confirmation of achievements, Peacocks won't feel as much need to promote themselves.

With Peacock subordinates, keep careful track of things that are done well—projects that worked. Use this information to delegate in the future: "Because you did so well on the such-and-such project, I thought you'd be perfect for this." If you plan carefully, provide the kinds of work assignments your Peacocks are best suited for, and use sincere encouragement with them, Peacock productivity will probably improve.

Strategy 5: When questioning Peacocks, be thorough but not antagonistic.

In your frustration, you may feel like blasting Peacocks with, "I'm sick of you thinking you know it all. Just SHUT UP!" But common sense should tell you to keep quiet. Challenging Peacocks directly is rarely productive. In any confrontational situation, plan your questions carefully. Thoroughly present your position without placing blame. Rather than assume you know the entire situation, *ask* and see what new information comes to light. Peacocks act super-knowledgeable and secure, but they are neither. When you don't force Peacocks to confront their weaknesses, they're less likely to become defensive and protective. You'll get both better productivity and better attitudes.

Challenging Peacocks directly is rarely productive.

2

Strategy 6: Be accurate when presenting information to Peacocks.

As we saw in Strategy 5, Peacocks don't respond well to flimsy allegations or unsupported beliefs. Because they need to keep their own egos afloat, acknowledging yours isn't their concern. Interject your facts smoothly into conversation, as needed. Just don't hit Peacocks over the head with them. Although you might want to convince Peacocks, it's not worth your effort, since you'll get better productivity and cooperation from Peacocks when you recognize you can't win the ego battle.

Strategy 7: Give Peacocks responsibility, but hold them accountable.

While Peacocks are masters of using excuses to avoid responsibility, when you delegate, you *can* expect results. If the desired outcomes don't appear, use the nonconfrontational Strategies 5 and 6 to find out why. If the situation warrants, follow company policies that support termination of workers when supervisors document a string of mishandled projects that were appropriately delegated and defined. Obviously, you'd prefer that Peacocks produce, but you don't have to put up with people who simply don't do the work. Because Peacocks are also least likely to accept dismissal gracefully, make sure your documentation is in order.

Strategy 8: Don't confuse a Peacock supervisor's position with the behavior or style.

Your supervisor's job description is to give you direction and oversee your progress. If your supervisor also has an ego the size of Atlanta, that's not the boss talking, that's the Peacock. There's no reason to resent a supervisor's requests unless they are given in a demeaning or harsh way. Then your job may feel like a trap. Separate personality from position, and your head will be clearer when directives come your way. You may find it helpful to recognize that this Peacock will probably not be your boss forever, especially if your career moves you into another job. Keep in mind that every supervisor brings useful learning opportunities to you, even if some circumstances aren't as pleasant as others. In any case, find something good in the experience and appreciate its benefit to you.

Separate personality from position, and your head will be clearer when directives come your way.

Take a Moment

Now that you know several strategies for success in dealing with Peacocks, identify one Peacock coworker and two strategies you can employ to improve your interactions.

Peacock Coworker   Success Strategy

_____   _____

                                   _____

                                   Success Strategy

                                   _____

                                   _____

Next, identify a Peacock boss or subordinate and two strategies you can use to improve your interactions.

Peacock Boss/Subordinate   Success Strategy

_____   _____

                                   _____

                                   Success Strategy

                                   _____

                                   _____

2

Self-Check: Chapter Two Review

Answers to these questions appear on page 97.

1. True or False?
   There are two major types of Peacocks: those who temporarily feel puffed up about an actual achievement and those who regularly inflate any small success.

2. What are four difficult Peacock behaviors?

   a. _____

   b. _____

   c. _____

   d. _____

3. Listen to a Peacock (circle one):   MORE   LESS

4. True or False?
   It's important to be thorough with Peacocks. Face them with documentation and facts.

Chapter *Three*

Snails: They Stall on Decision Making

Chapter Objectives

▶ Appreciate dynamics that confound the Snail.

▶ Identify ways that stallers slip out of decision making.

▶ Determine which strategies work best with Snails.

Case Study

Rod glowered at Lamont and Patty, his department's two Snails. He didn't really like escargot, but these two coworkers were holding back the product he managed, and he was angry enough to eat them alive.

"How will we ever get this on the market if you don't get moving!" Rod yelled at Patty in a meeting. Patty explained that the packaging wasn't finished because one consultant's extensive research showed that the color scheme was an antiselling mix while another consultant said the colors would shoot sales through the roof. "At some point you'll have to take a chance!" shouted Rod. "And that point is now. Are we going to use it or redesign it?"

Patty hemmed and hawed, her face contorting as though she was struggling on a tightrope. "We'll go with it as is," she burst out like a gush of steam.

Rod looked at her in surprise. "What caused you to make up your mind?" he asked.

"Well," offered Patty, "Ann says the consultant who approved of it has a better track record of success."

"I should have known," Rod thought with disgust. Ann, Patty's secretary, was doing the job for her. Rod turned to Lamont. "What about you? Is the sales plan in place?"

"I think so," said Lamont. "I'm talking with some of the other sales managers to see if they like the commission plan."

"Why ask *them?*" Rod asked. "This is a whole new division. They don't sell anything like this."

"I still wanted their input," said Lamont.

"So, are you ready to go?" asked Rod.

"Not really," Lamont responded. "I need to get more information before we actually go to the salespeople with the kickoff, incentives, and all that."

3

Rod sighed, feeling he'd waited long enough. "How much more time do you need?"

Lamont shrugged. "I really don't know—some."

"*Some* more time?" Rod barked. "You've already missed two deadlines! Have your plan ready tomorrow!"

Without being mean or forceful, Snails can make you steam in frustration. Snails don't like making decisions—even simple ones. Because decisions often mean conflict, Snails prefer to crawl away. But Snail behavior can be an unproductive drag on the whole system, since decisions must be made regularly and their outcomes reach far and wide.

> **Because decisions often mean conflict, Snails prefer to crawl away.**

If you have Snail subordinates, you may feel as if you're facing a cement wall when delegating work, unless you help your Snails become more comfortable with making decisions. Yes, you will need to help your Snails relax with decision making. Saying, "You need to learn how to make decisions!" will only create more anxiety in these already cautious people. The strategies for success given in this chapter can help you guide the Snail toward better decision-making skills.

Recognizing Snail Behavior

Like all other workplace animals, Snails have both good qualities and bad. In trying to do their best, wanting to do the right thing, and seeking to work in harmony, Snails can bring pleasant attitudes, solid effort, and positive energy to your team. However, Snail characteristics can go astray in the following ways:

Snails don't like to make decisions.

Decisions reflect someone's opinion becoming reality. For example, if you believe your organization should use a certain kind of silicon chip while your peer believes you should use another, and you choose yours, you're saying, "I'll take the risk that my choice is more appropriate for this task." While each worker carries part of the responsibility for a company's total success, making such a specific decision adds personal responsibility for a particular product's achievement—which definitely frightens our Snails.

The bigger the decision, the more agony Snails feel. For them, choosing between two good job offers can be like pulling a molar without Novocaine. Snails would never think, "Look at that! My skills are so good I've gained the right to choose between two excellent opportunities." Instead Snails panic, thinking, "Oh, no! How will I ever make the right decision?" Over time, Snails learn to avoid decision-making situations. Now, they need encouragement to improve these skills.

Snails often avoid decisions about their workload, making others pick up the slack.

Snails don't decide to stall as a way to cut their workload. Their workload gets trimmed as a result of their idling and fearful habits.

Snails aren't lazy by nature, but they've learned to avoid conflict-producing situations. With enough strong people in a department, Snails may do very well. Aggressive and ambitious coworkers often prefer taking the reins of a project from Snails, thinking, "It's easy for me to make decisions, so I'll just go ahead." Others might manipulate Snails for personal gain, and if decisions can be avoided, Snails may accept the influence. Snails don't decide to stall as a way to cut their workload. Their workload gets trimmed as a result of their idling and fearful habits.

34

Because Snails are reluctant to take action, fast-movers can rush ahead of them, leaving Snails with fewer accomplishments to show. While trying to reduce blame in their work lives, Snails don't take risks, and without taking some risk, they don't receive much glory. In today's rapid-fire workplace, Snail-like stalling means others must absorb the work of those who are stuck in "idle." As a result, Snails are often found in lower-level jobs. The ability to make decisions is so crucial to being a leader that a lack of this capacity can prevent career promotions.

While trying to reduce blame in their work lives, Snails don't take risks, and without taking some risk, they don't receive much glory.

Snails are afraid to disappoint others.

That's why decision making is so challenging for them. But they end up being a disappointment anyway because they can't make decisions! It's a sad cycle. Many Snails grew up in homes where they were belittled, always told their decisions were wrong, or made to feel that they were a disappointment. This not only stifled their enthusiasm but also made them dependent upon pleasing others.

Snails want to do what's *right,* which may not be the most productive choice.

Although Snails aren't bad, as we might characterize headstrong bullies, their sense of wanting to do what's right can create problems in the workplace.

■ Snail Charles knew when he took the job that he'd be involved in managing the company's manufacturing process. To save transportation costs and stave off fierce industry competition, the CEO decided to use a lake near their rural location for disposal of water-soluble, nontoxic waste, since the county had no dumping ban in place. Company scientists believed the waste material was biodegradable, but only time would tell.

Although his background could shed more light on the dumping activity, Charles didn't approach the CEO. Since the dumping began, however, Charles became more distressed. When coworker Penelope pressed him about it, Charles explained his feelings. She found Charles had good points, with scientific soundness, but he refused to go to the CEO.

When Penelope and a few others decided to challenge the CEO about the dumping activity, she asked for Charles's help. "I don't know . . .," he mumbled. "I don't want to disappoint

3

you, but I don't want to go up against him, either." Charles couldn't decide, and finally Penelope said, "We're going to the CEO this afternoon, with or without you." While at home for lunch, Charles called the department secretary, saying he'd become sick and wouldn't be returning to work that day.

The CEO's approach may sound like nothing more than the harsh reality of business, but Charles's response shows how Snails can be overly influenced by externals. Highways would never be built by Snails because they wouldn't want to move people out of their homes. Canals would never be dug with Snails in charge because they wouldn't want to make anyone dig a ditch. Snails are not so much sensitive people as they are reluctant to challenge others directly, which takes a willingness to make decisions. Snails prefer to "wait out" a situation by idling, as if they can avoid involvement while circumstances occur around them.

Snails tend to be perfectionists.

Wanting to do their best for everyone is an admirable Snail quality. But when doing their best becomes a search for perfection or if everyone encompasses too many people, Snails waste much of their promise and effort on impossibilities.

Snails don't want to be unpopular.

Strong leaders need to make wise choices, but Snails don't want to recognize that sometimes the best solution may not be a popular one.

Strong leaders need to make wise choices, but Snails don't want to recognize that sometimes the best solution may not be a popular one. Snails often make severe compromises in order to avoid offending anyone. Snails may think they're popular because they don't disappoint anyone with their decisions, but in truth they're not popular at all because they can't make *sound* decisions.

Take a Moment

Think back on your exchanges with Snail personalities. What statements did they make that revealed a need to please, to avoid conflict, or to seek popularity with everyone?

Name   **Statement(s)**

_____   _____

                             _____

_____   _____

                             _____

_____   _____

                             _____

3

Dealing Successfully with Snails

Don't let snails get the better of you. Follow these 10 strategies to deal successfully with Snail behavior.

Strategy 1: Carefully outline the work to be done, set a deadline, and get Snails to agree.

Provide Snails with full information, and get their agreement to do specific work by a set deadline. If you don't get the requested output from Snail subordinates because they can't make decisions, help them improve this capacity by requiring that they attend training in areas of leadership skills, time management, and decision making.

Strategy 2: Ask Snails how they feel, and encourage them to voice unspoken concerns.

Remember that Snails can be very frustrated, even if they don't easily make decisions. Because Snails naturally delay and avoid making up their minds, they may also be reluctant to express themselves aloud. You can help by providing a format or safe outlet. Showing Snails that you do care about their progress reduces their level of anxiety and eases their internal conflict, especially about decision making.

Strategy 3: Ask Snails for a detailed plan with specific steps toward the completion of a project.

Some Snails fear they're doing everything wrong and become paralyzed. Recognizing that each item is only a small part of the whole can help Snails better decide how to move ahead one way or another. Your step-by-step discussion will help Snails see their pieces as parts of a larger picture. Besides, your friendly discussion about their work provides Snails with reassurance that they really are on the right path.

Strategy 4: Use numeric-based measurements to reach answers.

Even if Snails aren't making the actual decision, just knowing that their information will affect critical situations can make them reluctant to share. Asking them either open-ended or closed-ended questions will not prompt them to speak. Instead think of ways you can help Snails be specific.

Rather than asking, "What'd you think of that?" ask, "If you had to rank her know-how on a scale of 1 to 10, with 1 being lowest and 10 being highest, where would you rank it?" Be aware: Smart Snails will sigh and say, "I don't know. There's no way I can rank her ability!" To which you reply, "Don't worry about whether you really know. Rank it according to how you see it at this point. Just throw out a number."

Forcing Snails to speed up their thinking process gives them less time to put up defensive barriers.

Forcing Snails to speed up their thinking process gives them less time to put up defensive barriers. By framing your request in terms of numbers, you remove some of their decision-making trauma. Even then, you may need to ask for the same information in two or three ways before Snails will quantify their position. Other measurement-oriented questions may be, "What would you say is the average?" or "Is this a 50/50 deal?" As much as possible, frame your requests within numerical formulas.

Strategy 5: Improve communication with Snails to help lower everyone's frustration level.

Open the lines of communication between you and your Snail coworkers, subordinates, and superiors. Improving two-way communication helps with most difficult people and situations, and it is certainly useful when dealing with Snails. While better communication may not specifically help your Snails' decision-making abilities, you will learn more about how to get the information you need from them.

Strategy 6: Verbally support Snails' decisions whenever they're made.

3

Since Snails take time and (massive) effort to make their decisions, verbally support them. Don't say, "Finally, you made a decision." Instead say, "It's good that you came to your decision." You don't have to say it was the right decision—just compliment the decision-making process. If you supervise Snails, pay attention when they make their decisions, or they're likely to think: "Why'd I bother? No one really cares!"

> **You don't have to say a Snail made the right decision—just compliment the decision-making process.**

Strategy 7: Break large decisions or projects into smaller pieces.

The decision-making process loses some of its terror for Snails when it's dismantled into smaller, easier sections. Start with small items, gradually increasing their scope and difficulty.

Especially When You're Supervised By Snails:

Strategy 8: Remind Snails that Time = Money.

Snail bosses might aggravate you to the core, making you analyze something to death or repeatedly delaying a project start date. But don't attack your Snail boss. Without using the exact words, you can offer gentle reminders that time equals money.

Instead of saying, "We're way past deadline!" you can suggest, "Maybe we've devoted enough of our energy to this; it could be time to wrap this up and pass it along now." Instead of saying, "I don't want to work on this anymore! I'm sick of it," you can say, "Is this project the best use of my time right now? Should I move on to something more urgent?"

Strategy 9: Use the concept of "good enough," especially if Snail bosses are perfectionists.

You can say, "Perhaps we've done enough on this project—it's passed all our benchmarks." You are subtly making the decision to *finish*. Or you can say, "The quality we have here is the top of our industry," meaning it's *good enough*. Someone has to make decisions to keep a project moving, and even if Snails won't, your diplomatic questions and statements can benefit the process.

Strategy 10: Frequently reassert your dedication to the supervisor and the company.

Gently remind
Snail bosses
of your
appreciation
for their
abilities, and
state your
support for the
goals of the
organization.

While you may wish you could take matters into your own hands and move ahead, remember that your supervisor is still your supervisor. Gently remind Snail bosses of your appreciation for their abilities, and state your support for the goals of the organization. Above all, don't engage a Snail boss in a contest of wills; when Snail bosses' egos are intact, they can exemplify a more egalitarian approach to workplace decision making.

Take a Moment

Now that you know several strategies for success in dealing with Snails, identify one Snail coworker and two strategies you can employ to improve your interactions.

Snail Coworker

Success Strategy

_____

_____

_____

Success Strategy

_____

_____

Next, identify a Snail boss or subordinate and two strategies you can use to improve your interactions.

Snail Boss or Subordinate   Success Strategy

_____

_____

_____

Success Strategy

_____

_____

3

Self-Check: Chapter Three Review

Answers to these questions appear on page 98.

1. Snails (circle one):
   DO / DO NOT like making decisions.

2. To get results with Snails, carefully outline the work to be

   done, set a _____,

   and get Snails to _____.

3. True or False?
   Using numeric-based or other systems requiring specificity
   will get a better response from Snails.

4. True or False?
   Breaking larger projects into smaller pieces will help Snails
   get the work done.

Chapter *Four*
Vipers: They Attack from Behind

Chapter Objectives

▶ Appreciate the aggression behind Viper behavior.

▶ Learn standard Viper retorts that can make you look like the difficult person.

▶ Determine which strategies work best with Vipers.

Case Study

Lynn dreaded the weekly departmental meeting. She'd recently been promoted, and she knew Russ resented it. Russ was a true Viper: He always had several things to say at every meeting—but only under his breath.

As the meeting began, Lynn outlined the new project. It wouldn't be easy, but at least the work was shared. Russ whispered loudly to the coworker next to him, "Hmm, let's see if this will really get done, or if this is just more of management's dreaming." Although she heard him, Lynn ignored Russ's comment.

As the travel portion of the project was outlined, Lynn overheard Russ say, "If I were her, I'd set it up that way too—and send myself to Florida." As the meeting ended and the conversation become more casual, staff members mentioned a school event. Russ turned to Lynn and smirked as he left. "I'll bet you were teacher's pet when you were in school," he said.

Later Lynn confided in her close friend and coworker Karen. "I'm sick of his sniping. It's too bad Russ didn't get promoted, but with his behavior, that's not possible now."

"Why don't you talk with him about it?" Karen suggested.

"I don't want to," answered Lynn. "It's *his* problem. Let him deal with it!"

If, like Lynn, you refuse to confront a Viper, you won't achieve good results. Letting Vipers fester in their nests of resentment always ends up with your getting bitten. Vipers have serious issues, but they can't address them directly. Instead, they would rather slither around, hissing to others in underhanded ways. Although you might prefer to ignore their biting remarks, it's not wise simply to hope Vipers will disappear.

> **Vipers have serious issues, but they can't address them directly.**

But be careful. If you crack down on them, you may appear overbearing or receive standard Viper retorts: "You're just too sensitive," or "Can't you take a joke?" Remember that this is Viper aggression in disguise, although it's hard to recognize. Vipers' primary negative behavior is that they attack from behind, using innuendoes and snide remarks.

Keep in mind that Vipers are like all other workplace animals who have good qualities and bad. Many started their working careers with good intentions and actually produced fine work. Unfortunately, because they found it difficult to accept praise or compliments, they were unprepared for direct recognition or rewards.

4

To cover their embarrassment, they may have responded in off-hand ways, leading people to think they really didn't need recognition, which began a vicious cycle that kept them from receiving additional positive regard. So now Vipers resort to sarcasm, innuendo, and sniping. Their comments can have value, like an early warning system, because their troublesome statements may actually hide thorny issues that no one in the company wants to confront.

In this chapter, you'll find strategies to help you work with Vipers. If you practice the strategies, you can expect that Viper behavior will change, at least around you. Vipers *will* back down when dealt with effectively, making it possible to supervise, work with, and achieve more productivity from Vipers too.

Recognizing Viper Behavior

Like Peacocks, Vipers suffer from low self-esteem. While the Peacock lack of self-esteem displays itself as *too much* talking, Viper lack of self-esteem means they *don't* speak up directly. When Vipers' sniping behavior appears, there are often a variety of reasons.

Vipers feel they don't have control over their lives.

If you hear them say anything, you generally hear comments like, "There's nothing I can do about it," or "That's just the way things are." Vipers see little chance to change their own lives or to make things better: workplaces tell them how to work; the world tells them how to live. Vipers feel the only effect they can have is to make sniping remarks from the background.

Vipers suspect or even fear they will fail.

Many Vipers
want to try
and wish they
could do an
outstanding
job, but they
start from a
feeling that
they will fail.

Although you may see that a new project or challenge would brighten your life, Vipers see it as a formidable new foe. Many Vipers want to try and wish they could do an outstanding job, but they start from a feeling that they will fail. Some Vipers even make failure a self-fulfilling prophecy: They start out fearing they will fail, they work from this basis of fear, and when they *do* fail, they say to themselves, "Well, I knew I'd fail." Other Vipers don't actually fail very often, but they have trouble remembering their successes. By magnifying mistakes and shortcomings, they perceive more failure than they truly have.

Vipers have difficulty accepting praise or compliments.

Have you ever complimented people who drop their heads and mumble, "Oh, it was nothing." You feel like straightening out their slumping shoulders and saying, "Yes, it *was* something! That's why I'm complimenting you!" Vipers have a tough time accepting these good words. Perhaps they've dealt with so much criticism in their lives, it's hard for them to believe others are truly impressed by what they do.

Vipers feel powerless to make choices, and therefore, let others decide.

While others may meet with the boss one by one to hash out raises, Vipers will be much happier if the boss says, "You get X percentage, and that's it. We can't pay more." Vipers' feelings of powerlessness are also revealed in their difficulty making decisions, even in noncritical situations. If the gang from work goes to lunch and someone asks a Viper to choose the location, the reply is likely to be, "Oh, I don't care. You decide."

Vipers criticize others from the background.

While this is the predominant behavior of Vipers, you should be able to see that such sniping often stems from several internal conflicts and fears. Just recognize that even if Vipers don't want to make choices, they feel free to criticize the choice you make and will usually make snide remarks to others under their breath.

Dealing Successfully with Vipers

Most people deal with Vipers by pretending they didn't hear them or ignoring the behavior. But this can make you look weak, especially in a group. If you're a forceful person, perhaps you've tried bulldozing your way over their whispered statements. But don't expect that you can push Vipers so far that they'll speak up directly. You're better off to build a rapport with your Vipers, using the following five strategies for success. Each is explored in detail.

> **Ignoring Vipers' bad behavior can make you look weak, especially in a group.**

4

Strategy 1: Address Viper behavior openly, especially if you're sniped at in a group setting.

Although many difficult behaviors should be addressed in private, such an approach is not effective with Vipers, because they need an audience to do their sniping. When you hear Vipers whisper their caustic remarks, take immediate action with a direct statement, such as one of the following:

◆ "Please repeat your comment, (person's name). I didn't hear you."

◆ "Perhaps that's something you should be telling me in private."

◆ "Did I hear you say that (Viper's remark)?"

Your point is not to humiliate Vipers, but to let them know that:

◆ You will not tolerate whispered backbiting.

◆ There is little or no basis in fact to their comments.

Strategy 2: Involve others, if necessary.

Vipers will freely snipe in a group, but they will be shocked if you openly involve others who are present. You'll be very effective at stopping Viper attacks if you ask a different person in the group to comment on Viper remarks, as in, "How about that, Howie? Do you agree with (Viper)?"

Strategy 3: Persist. Be direct even if Vipers continue to be indirect.

If the sniping remarks are about work, your skills, or other important issues and you challenge them directly, Vipers may retort a few minutes later with quiet remarks about personal characteristics, such as your clothes or hair. Don't shrug this off just because the aim of the remark has changed. Vipers use these ploys to test the waters.

> **You must continue to address the sniping behavior, even if the points Vipers make seem trivial.**

If you try to ignore the comments or are half-hearted in your response, Viper sarcasm and innuendo about bigger issues will resurface. You must continue to address the sniping behavior, even if the points Vipers make seem trivial. The successful strategy is to break the pattern of sniping comments, regardless of the content of the remarks.

Strategy 4: Confront typical Viper retorts by avoiding sarcasm and emphasizing the truth.

When you address Vipers and get comments like, "You're just too sensitive," calmly respond with a remark such as, "No, I'm not too sensitive. I'm interested in the truth behind your statement." Vipers also battle challenges with, "Can't you take a joke?" to which you can respond with, "But that didn't sound like a joke. What's the real issue you'd like to address?" Vipers often truly have serious complaints or problems about particular subjects, but they don't know how to address them in forthright ways. Because Vipers often feel powerless to make changes and don't feel anyone will honestly listen to and address their concerns, they resort to snide comments and whispered remarks.

Strategy 5: Don't let down your guard. Continue to challenge Viper behavior.

Sometimes, Vipers back down after several days of using these strategies, but the behavior soon erupts again. Because sniping is such an ingrained pattern with Vipers, you'll need to be consistent and persistent in continually addressing their negative behavior.

Take a Moment

Now that you know several strategies for success in dealing with Vipers, identify one Viper coworker and two strategies you can employ to improve your interactions.

Viper Coworker   Success Strategy

_____   _____

                        _____

                        Success Strategy

                        _____

                        _____

Next, identify a Viper boss or subordinate and two strategies you can use to improve your interactions.

Viper Boss or Subordinate Success Strategy

_____   _____

                        _____

                        Success Strategy

                        _____

                        _____

4

49

Self-Check: Chapter Four Review

Answers to these questions appear on page 98.

1. True or False?
   Vipers' caustic remarks and innuendoes are actually aggressive behavior in disguise.

2. Viper self-esteem is (circle one):   LOW   HIGH

3. If you challenge Viper remarks, two very common responses aimed to disarm you may be:

   _____

   _____

   _____

4. True or False?
   Directly addressing Viper remarks one time is almost never enough. Vipers will test the waters and attack again.

Chapter *Five*

Tigers: They Come On Strong

Chapter Objectives

▶ Appreciate the Tiger's past, present, and future role in management.

▶ Learn to confront Tigers without provoking conflict.

▶ Determine which strategies work best with Tigers.

Case Study

"I've moved the Monday morning meeting to 8:00 a.m.," Edgar announced, but there were no audible groans from his subordinates at the table. They didn't dare make a sound. Although the regular workday was scheduled to run from 8:30 a.m. to 5:00 p.m., Edgar had convinced everyone they had to work late, and now he was taking an extra half-hour of their time first thing in the morning.

Like everyone else in the room, Lance chalked it up to the start of another bad day. But the Tiger hadn't stopped growling. "Lance, you're flying to Boston tomorrow to meet with the Aerosonic people," Edgar announced. "They need our help."

"But what about the Timlane project?" Lance began. "It needs . . ."

"I've already put Sarah on that," Edgar interrupted. Lance grit his teeth, recalling the enormous amount of effort he'd put into the Timlane project. Now Sarah would get credit because she'd be there for the finale. To make matters worse, the Aerosonic clients didn't really need him on site. The last two times he'd visited, they'd even said, "Why don't we teleconference our next meeting? You don't have to fly all the way out here." But when Lance shared Aerosonic's comment, Edgar boomed, "That's not how we treat clients!"

Lance wanted to remain in town for more than just the Timlane project. In Edgar's office after the meeting, Lance carefully explained, "Edgar, tomorrow is my anniversary. My wife and I planned a special dinner, and we have tickets to the theater. If I have to fly to Boston, couldn't I at least leave a day later?"

"You know work comes first," Edgar warned sternly. "Aerosonic is your client, and you have to take care of them. If you don't want to do your job right, just let me know. I'm sure Sarah would be glad to take over."

Later, Kate stopped by Lance's office. She'd been the object of Edgar's wrath in the past and appreciated how Lance felt. "You should do something about it," said Kate. "He knows you don't really need to go to Boston. He should cut you some slack."

"Forget it," said Lance. "I'm not going to do battle with him again."

"You, know, sometimes I think we spend as much time and energy trying to manage Edgar as we do performing our jobs!" Kate observed, and Lance nodded in agreement.

5

Take a Moment

Think back to clashes you've had with Tigers in your workplace. How did you respond?

Physical sensations: _____

_____

Thoughts: _____

_____

Reply/Replies: _____

_____

Tiger's response: _____

_____

Recognizing Tiger Behavior

In earlier, more hierarchical workplaces, Tigers were often valued employees. Tigers were usually men who growled, showed their claws and teeth, and got things done. Employees knew where they stood with a Tiger: They either obeyed or were eaten. Because it generated results, Tigers' aggressive behavior frequently brought them promotions to top management positions.

Tiger traits can still be valuable when companies are in the difficult start-up stage, where lots of hard work is required and workers need solid direction. Tiger behavior can also be helpful in limited situations, such as when handling a difficult employee or straightening out a department that's full of waste and incompetence.

Tiger behavior is outdated now that we're deep into the Information Age.

But for the most part, Tiger behavior is outdated now that we're deep into the Information Age, with its emphasis on clear communication, constant interaction, and mutual exchange. Unfortunately, though its day may have passed, Tiger behavior still exists, and you may find yourself needing to work with a Tiger without getting eaten for lunch. But like other workplace animals, Tigers can be handled if you recognize that their behavior can go astray in the following ways:

Tigers will prey on you if you let them.

Tigers have no trouble taking advantage of you, getting information from you, taking credit for what you've done, or just humiliating you, if that's necessary. They are so goal-oriented and/or egotistical, they'll run over people like bulldozers and may lie, cheat, or take other unethical steps to get what they want.

Will they feel guilty? No. Tigers have the attitude that, "It's just business," or "That's just part of the job." Although it may seem inconsistent to others, Tigers may be kind to people in their neighborhood because that's what's expected by society, while on the job, they'll yell at coworkers because "the work has to get done."

Tigers can easily disrespect you.

Tigers expect you to prove yourself—or suffer their disrespect. But you don't need to crumble at this Tiger approach. First, know that you deserve respect, even if Tigers don't want to give it. Second, don't assume that because Tigers act strong, they are better than you. Tigers *should* respect you, and they *will*; they just don't do it automatically or openly.

Tigers respect those who are logical, sensible, and calmly stand their ground.

You may think that if you fight with a Tiger and win, you'll receive their respect. Not so. In reality, you cannot "win" a screamfest. Tigers don't lose to someone else's anger; they just dig in their heels and fight to the death. While you won't receive their respect instantly, you can earn it with calmly presented facts, consistently good work, proven productivity, and demonstrations of good common sense.

> You can earn Tiger respect with calmly presented facts, consistently good work, proven productivity, and demonstrations of good common sense.

5

Tigers are ready to clash anytime, anywhere.

Don't think you'll get the best of them on a "down day" or convince them of something they don't want by "wearing them down." Tigers prefer to dominate and are always ready for conflict. If need be, they may even create an upheaval. Don't waste time planning a confrontation you can't win. Be aware of Tiger tendencies and take another approach.

Tigers may have many problems away from work.

Don't be surprised if you learn that Tigers have trouble with spouses or children, with neighbors, or even at their church or synagogue. Don't be startled to discover that Tigers have been fired from other jobs or otherwise forced out. Although Tigers can treat work and home as two separate arenas, some are so often at the boiling point, they only see the world as one big Super Bowl—which they need to win.

Tigers have a need to feel they're "right."

It doesn't matter whether they are or not. Their behavior is fueled by their ego, which says, "You're always right." So how do Tigers differ from Peacocks? Peacocks think they know it all.

55

Tigers don't necessarily think they know it *all;* they just think they know more than *you.* A sense of superiority is what's most important to Tigers.

Tigers are highly impatient.

In a rush to get things done, Tigers expect people to cooperate (meaning "obey") and produce. If Tigers don't produce, it's only because they clash with people so much that others don't work well with them. Even when Tigers want to "get things done—now," their impatience can block true progress rather than push it forward, leading to missed goals and low productivity.

Tigers are workaholics, so they often move up in the organization.

Don't be surprised when Tigers are promoted. Those in the upper levels of management may not recognize the full impact of Tiger behavior. They only see work getting done and people being managed. If you supervise a Tiger, don't fear that you'll be overlooked for promotions because such a hard-charger works for you. Make sure you harness Tiger desire to work hard. Use facts to stay one step ahead of your Tigers. Channel their energies in productive ways, and you'll keep them from harming others in your department with their aggressive behavior.

Channel Tiger energies in productive ways, and you'll keep them from harming others in your department with their aggressive behavior.

Dealing Successfully with Tigers

You don't need a whip and a chair to work with a Tiger. Follow these nine strategies for success with Tiger behavior.

Strategy 1: Use eye contact and strong body language in your interactions.

Take a deep breath and relax before you meet or speak with Tigers. Purposely hold eye contact. In conversation, pull back your shoulders and stand strong, even if you feel like you're losing the argument.

While you may need to practice being aware of your eye contact and body language during your first few Tiger interactions, over time, you'll become more comfortable with this stance. Obviously, each person with whom you deal requires a specific approach. Let your sensitivity be your guide, and you won't stand up to a Snail as you must with a Tiger.

Strategy 2: Be firm with Tigers, but don't invite head-on collisions.

Simply ask for what you want as straightforwardly as possible. Be direct and to the point, but keep your tone even and your temper calm. Although Tigers may seem always ready to fight, if you don't invite trouble through your approach, you won't encourage problems. Always be prepared with a calm counter statement.

If you've made your request and the Tiger begins to do battle, say, "We don't need to get into all of that right now. We must get back to work." Then move on, even if you don't get the information you need right then. If the Tiger follows and says, "You're always chickening out," or "You can't stand up to me," know that by refusing to fight, you're standing up for yourself in your own way. Realize that you can calmly approach the Tiger again, as many times at it takes to get what you need.

Rather than ignore an interruption or ask Tigers not to interrupt, make a direct statement to them, such as, "You interrupted me," and maintain strong eye contact. If you waffle and ask, "Could you stop interrupting me?" or say, "It bothers me when you interrupt me," Tigers think you really mean "you hurt my feelings," a position for which they have no sympathy.

Strategy 3: Don't use sarcasm, poke fun, or try to make jokes with Tigers.

Especially if your humor leans toward sarcasm, you'll find it easy to make smart remarks in conversation with Tigers. If you don't feel confident enough to tackle the real issues and use sarcasm as a way to deal with aggressive people, or if you aren't mature enough to handle the situation in a well-planned, even-handed way, you'll just irritate Tigers, who may then become more aggressive toward you. Likewise, trying to soften the situation with a joke or subtle humor also will not work. Tigers see this as impurity penetrating the all-important Work to Get Done. While most people can do their work and still have a laugh, that's not common behavior for Tigers.

> **Although Tigers may seem always ready to fight, if you don't invite trouble through your approach, you won't encourage problems.**

5

Strategy 4: Don't assume Tigers are right just because they're forceful.

Tigers always think they're right—and they add a heaping spoonful of aggressiveness to help you swallow it. But don't bite. Don't confuse forcefulness with validity. Might does not make right. Conversely, though, see the next strategy.

> **Don't confuse forcefulness with validity. Might does not make right.**

Strategy 5: Don't assume Tigers are wrong just because they always think they're right.

Once you've developed defenses against Tigers, you may feel safe in assuming, "Here they go again, all hot air," or assuming that their egos are all that's driving them. But Tigers want to and do generate actual results and reach high achievements. During those activities, they've learned many useful things and have achieved some great things. Tigers aren't always wrong just because they're loud. Recognize the valuable contributions they have made and can make.

Take a Moment

Review your Tiger encounters, and identify your responses to the following situations:

When a Tiger, assumed to be right, was actually wrong:

_____

_____

_____

_____

When a Tiger was forceful and assumed wrong, but was actually right:

_____

_____

_____

_____

Strategy 6: Be calm and direct about not liking Tiger behavior.

Your approach to this strategy depends on whether you're a Tiger coworker, superior, or subordinate. While you don't have to tiptoe around your Tigers, remember that clashing head-to-head isn't the right approach, either. Your relationship will help you decide the smoothest way to explain that certain behavior is unacceptable.

Don't drag your statements out and invite an argument. State your dislike for the behavior (not the person) and move on to something else. If the Tiger retorts, say that you can't discuss it now because you have other business at hand. While this might be difficult if the Tiger is your boss, in such a case, you can gently state, "That's all I needed to say right now. I don't believe we need to take up the issue here. It's not a good use of our time."

> **State your dislike for the behavior (not the person) and move on to something else.**

Here's another example. During a meeting, the Tiger yelled at you forcefully, and it was quite embarrassing, even for the other people in the room. Although you didn't do anything wrong, the Tiger's temper was overwhelming. Depending on your job level, here are ways you could respond.

5

- **If a Tiger is your boss:** "You know, I want to do the best job I can for you. And I will. But if you feel strongly about that issue in the future, I'd rather hear your feelings on it in private, not in front of others at a meeting."

- **If a Tiger is your peer:** "I didn't feel it was necessary for you to talk to me that way in the meeting. Please don't speak to me that way again."

- **If you supervise a Tiger:** "Just so you know, your outburst at the meeting was unacceptable. I want to make our working relationship as positive as possible, but I will not tolerate that kind of behavior." (**Note:** You do not need to get agreement. Do not ask at the end of that statement, "Do you agree?" Expect Tigers to hear it, synthesize the information, and act differently in the future.)

With any such outburst of rude Tiger behavior, don't think, "I'm just going to drop it," or avoid the subject. Say something! (See Strategy 9.)

Strategy 7: Don't expect Tigers to change.

We dream of Tiger bosses encountering a life-changing experience, something to make them gentle and caring. Or we hope that Tiger coworkers will get another job. Don't waste time in idle dreams of such "ways out." Tigers will not change because you want them to. Learn to work around and with them.

Strategy 8: Don't get involved if Tigers ridicule or make fun of others.

While you practice setting your sarcasm aside, Tigers themselves may use sarcasm or outright derision toward others. Don't join in. You'll only support negative Tiger behavior.

Strategy 9: If you disagree, don't remain silent or Tigers assume you support their behavior.

Verbalize your disagreement matter-of-factly to show your lack of support.

With typical forcefulness, Tigers gather speed as they roll through life, insisting that their way is right. But if you disagree with an issue, if you know the behavior is wrong, or if you don't like what's being proposed, it's important for you to speak up. Remember, don't arm yourself for a clash. Verbalize your disagreement matter-of-factly to show your lack of support. When you speak up, you require Tigers to justify their actions and you demonstrate that unnecessary, undesired, and inappropriate behavior will not succeed.

Take a Moment

Now that you know several strategies for success in dealing with Tigers, identify one Tiger coworker and two strategies you can employ to improve your interactions.

Tiger Coworker   Success Strategy

_____   _____

                     _____

                     Success Strategy

                     _____

                     _____

Next, identify a Tiger boss or subordinate and two strategies you can use to improve your interactions.

Tiger Boss or Subordinate   Success Strategy

_____   _____

                     _____

                     Success Strategy

                     _____

                     _____

5

Self-Check: Chapter Five Review

Answers to these questions appear on page 98.

1. True or False?
   Under earlier management systems, the Tiger boss's behavior was valued.

2. True or False?
   To win against an aggressive person, be strong and go for head-to-head combat.

3. Tigers are (circle one):

   Alcoholics   Workaholics   Chocoholics

4. What type of body language is important when dealing with Tigers?

   _____

   _____

5. True or False?
   Don't remain silent when you disagree with a Tiger. It only makes things worse.

Chapter *Six*

Koala Bears: They're Too Agreeable

Chapter Objectives

▶ Distinguish between genuinely nice behavior and Koala Bear agreement-to-avoid-conflict behavior.

▶ Develop ways to be appropriately sociable while helping Koala Bears make decisions and increase productivity.

▶ Determine which strategies work best with Koala Bears.

Case Study

Phil came to work each day with a big smile on his face. "What a nice man," the office receptionist always said. But David didn't agree. Although he and Phil worked closely on many projects, David couldn't believe Phil was actually his workplace peer because he could work circles around Phil.

David could also see how Phil's super-sweet style interfered with sound department management. After all, David noted with disgust, Anne was still there. A filing clerk, she'd been reprimanded and put on probation for her many offenses, the last of which was coming back from lunch drunk! David was sure Phil's reprimands were not exactly stern.

In that morning's department planning meeting, Phil remarked about everyone's good work. But when discussion on one item heated up, Phil excused himself for the bathroom. David just shook his head, knowing Phil wouldn't be back before the meeting was over—Phil always hid when situations turned less than agreeable.

Phil's departure also meant that David was left to hand out new work assignments. But when it came to informing the staff about this weekend's mandatory overtime, David confronted Phil and said, "You do it! It's your turn." By the end of the day, however, Phil still hadn't told anyone about the overtime. When David asked him about it, Phil said, "I think tomorrow would be better for that. Maybe everyone's morale will be a little higher."

David grit his teeth, thinking, "I'll end up doing this, too, because Phil doesn't have the guts to be anything but Mr. Sweetness and Light!"

Remember that the qualities of all workplace animals only become difficult when they go overboard in one direction or another. While we most often equate difficult with negative, positive characteristics can also be overdone when they interfere with good work or disrupt productivity and daily interactions. If they're more concerned with avoiding conflict than maintaining productivity, Koala Bears like Phil can be a big challenge for both coworkers and supervisors.

Recognizing Koala Bear Behavior

Koala Bears are very sociable people who enjoy and derive energy from their interactions with others. In fact, when they're in the right jobs, Koala Bears generally demonstrate superior ways to handle other types of difficult people. They typically respond with kindness to every situation and can often maintain a positive outlook, even in the face of dire circumstances.

> When they're in the right jobs, Koala Bears generally demonstrate superior ways to handle other types of difficult people.

6

While any workplace can benefit from Koala Bear optimism, be certain they're not *always* looking at the world through rose-colored glasses, avoiding the hurdles that occasionally appear in their paths and obstructing necessary progress. Koala Bear behavior can also go astray because:

In the wrong job, Koala Bears' social nature can impede productivity.

When packing cartons in the back of the warehouse, Koala Bears will be very unhappy. But put them at the front desk and they'll brighten considerably. Because Koala Bears value social acceptance, they're not very shrewd about who they pick for office pals. Often, their need to be "the nicest person in the office" and their interest in social interaction hinders honest communication and hampers both their own productivity and that of others.

Koala Bears tend to waste time at work.

By talking too much, visiting too long with others, or extending lunch periods to be sociable, Koala Bears negatively affect their productivity and that of their peers, who end up doing more of the actual project work. If you supervise Koala Bears and attempt to explain how their socializing is excessive and inappropriate, they and their coworkers may see you as harsh. In reality, you may not be harsh at all. It's only the contrast between your request and Koala Bears' social needs that's truly dramatic.

Koala Bears don't deal well with conflict.

Somewhat surprisingly, Koala Bears can make decisions, even tough ones. They don't stall like Snails or keep quiet. But if the discussion becomes heated, they wilt like an orchid in a hog pen. You might think that Koala Bears' natural socializing would make them good salespeople. Not true. Koala Bears can't handle the built-in seller/buyer conflict of the sales process. After all, you can't sell people something when you concentrate primarily on being sweet to them.

> **Koala Bears can't handle the built-in seller/buyer conflict of the sales process.**

Dealing Successfully with Koala Bears

As you work your way through this book, you might feel you're being asked to extend extra effort and make major changes in your own behavior just to accommodate difficult people. But bursting forth with a verbal barrage about your frustration will only hinder progress with Koala Bears and other difficult people. In reality, you're learning to improve your interactions by being thoughtful about the behaviors you and your colleagues display. With awareness and practice, you'll soon eliminate wasted time and reduce your level of stress. Following are seven strategies for success with Koala Bear behavior.

Strategy 1: To build good relationships, interact informally with Koala Bears.

A foundation of friendliness will help if you delegate to Koala Bears or must work with them on teams or particular projects. If you've made the effort to establish a positive informal relationship, Koala Bears won't respond to firmness, specific deadlines, and hard work by feeling that you're being unfriendly.

Strategy 2: Because Koala Bears are insecure at heart, offer genuine compliments.

Look for successes, good traits, and other items you can compliment in Koala Bears from time to time. Because Koala Bears feed on positive interaction and the attention of others, your periodic nice words can help them feel more secure.

Take a Moment

What are some genuine compliments you can give Koala Bears in your life?

Name   Compliments

_____   _____

                              _____

_____   _____

                              _____

Strategy 3: Always take a nonthreatening approach to Koala Bears.

If you feel your temper flare, count to 10. If work isn't getting done, don't succumb to the temptation of warning Koala Bears that they'll be fired—unless it's the truth (and then, handle it gently). Koala Bears don't respond well to threats. If they seem to, fear has overtaken them. But remember that fearful people aren't productive—they soon cave in to stress, frustration, and resentment.

Koala Bears don't respond well to threats. If they seem to, fear has overtaken them.

Strategy 4: Clearly express your expectations, and hold Koala Bears accountable.

Although they don't say so out loud, many Koala Bears expect to be treated gently because they're so nice to others. Regardless of how nice they are, Koala Bears still need to produce as much as the other workers in their organizations. Brightening the workplace is no one's main duty. Be straightforward about the amount of work to be done, be clear about the requirements, and expect Koala Bears to comply.

6

Strategy 5: Emphasize that making mistakes is okay when we learn from them.

Because Koala Bears are often insecure and afraid of failure, they're afraid of making mistakes. As a result, they've learned to view success as friendliness and pleasant interaction instead of project-oriented accomplishment. Helping Koala Bears feel more secure with decisions and mistakes can improve their productivity. When you demonstrate by example that you know mistakes can be valuable parts of the learning process, not points for punishment, you help Koala Bears feel more comfortable with quantifiable effort.

> **Helping Koala Bears feel more secure with decisions and mistakes can improve their productivity.**

Strategy 6: Encourage Koala Bear assertiveness.

While you don't need to provide a crash course in hard reality, offering Koala Bears opportunities for training in assertiveness techniques can be of great benefit. Because Koala Bears are not naturally assertive, their people-oriented, agreement-based contacts often conflict with workplace requirements for productivity and accountability. Seminars, tapes, and books on assertiveness can help. If you're the supervisor, provide them. If you're a peer, suggest them—in a friendly way, so you won't offend. Ideally, you can create an opportunity to polish your own assertiveness techniques at the same time by saying to your Koala Bear peer, "See this? A seminar on assertiveness will be in our city soon. Let's go together."

Strategy 7: Demonstrate and use win/win concepts.

Since they seem to want agreement at all times, you might think Koala Bears are already in win/win mode. But Koala Bears tend to ignore problems, gloss over differences, and hide from conflict. Their perpetual pleasantness comes at the cost of recognizing and appreciating the true issues and reasons for discontent. Learning to create win/win situations helps Koala Bears improve their skills in negotiation, listening, and other beneficial techniques for successful interaction.

Take a Moment

Now that you know several strategies for success when dealing with Koala Bears, identify one Koala Bear coworker and two strategies you can employ to improve your interactions.

Koala Bear Coworker Success Strategy

_____ _____

         _____

         Success Strategy

         _____

         _____

Next, identify a Koala Bear boss or subordinate and two strategies you can use to improve your interactions.

Koala Boss or Subordinate Success Strategy

_____ _____

         _____

         Success Strategy

         _____

         _____

6

Self-Check: Chapter Six Review

Answers to these questions appear on page 99.

1. True or False?
   Being sociable with Koala Bears will help you get results.

2. Koala Bears tend to waste _____ at work.

3. True or False?
   To help Koala Bears make decisions and get work done instead of trying to remain "popular," demonstrate by your behavior that when we learn from them, making mistakes is okay.

4. True or False?
   You should clearly express your expectations to Koala Bears and hold them accountable.

Chapter *Seven*

Skunks: They Reek of Complaints and Negativity

Chapter Objectives

▶ Differentiate between temporary negative feelings and Skunks' continual complaining.

▶ Appreciate how Skunks influence others in unproductive ways.

▶ Determine which strategies work best with Skunks.

Case Study

"Look at Mark," Ted whispered to Mary. "He thinks he's so hot!" At the office holiday party, the new sales manager was making a little speech about how happy he is to join the company and how he feels it's a family. "Some family," Ted sulked aloud. "A abusive father and a dysfunctional mother."

"What do you mean?" asked Mary, confused.

"The CEO's a slave driver! Is he like family?" Ted asked. "And what about Olivia, the vice president? From what I hear, she's completely incompetent."

Mary was sick of Ted's complaining, but everyone was seated, and she couldn't easily get away from him. "Maybe Ted's just having a bad day," she thought, taking a bite of chocolate cake. But he continued.

"I don't know why we're even having a party," Ted whined. "What's to celebrate?"

Seeing the irony, Mary laughed and said, "Well, we can celebrate that we have jobs!"

Ted frowned. "We might not have jobs forever," he warned. "You know how things are these days."

"I just try to take one day at time," offered Mary, who was beginning to think that Ted might be incapable of looking at anything in a positive light.

With a bitter grin, Ted responded, "My take-home pay won't even take me home!"

"Oh, brother," Mary muttered to herself, "he's really on a roll."

"You'd think if they have the money to put together parties like this, they could fork over for bonuses," grumbled Ted. "But management wants all the money for themselves. You can bet they're getting a bonus this year."

"No one's getting a bonus. My supervisor told me," Mary asserted.

"That's what they tell you, but who knows what's really happening?" griped Ted.

"Not you, that's for sure," thought Mary. Suddenly she raised her hand, waved to someone across the room, and grabbed her plate. "I have to go see Rita. She must need to tell me something," she called over her shoulder as she left.

In a flash, Mary was gone, but Ted didn't think Rita motioned to Mary at all. "Nobody will give me the time of day," Ted muttered grimly. "What's the matter with these people?"

While many of us have occasional negative feelings about something in particular, those feelings are generally short-lived and fall into perspective when we look at our lives as a whole. Situations in the workplace can generate many of our negative feelings because we may feel we have less control over our work lives than we do over our personal lives. In the workplace, many circumstances can cause moods to turn sour, including:

7

◆ **Downsizing**—A fourth of your department is eliminated, and the supervisor tells you that the remaining employees will just have to pick up the slack.

◆ **Growth and competition**—Your company is not growing, while two competitors are expanding rapidly.

◆ **Money issues**—You learn that last year each employee got a $2,000 bonus, but this year there will be none.

Your workplace will suffer less negative behavior if you can describe it by any or all of the following characteristics:

◆ A dynamic organization with an air of vibrant energy, usually created by its good reputation, a strong and likable leader, and being part of a strong industry.

◆ Pay and benefits that are competitive and appropriate for the jobs available.

◆ A fair and equitable performance appraisal and evaluation system.

◆ A strong human resources department that maintains a well-defined hiring process, provides coaching and training, and monitors employee satisfaction.

What's Going On Here?

Skunks in the workplace often show themselves through dissatisfaction with the jobs they hold. Perhaps Skunks:

1. Took a job just to have an income rather than taking the time and effort to find what would give them greatest satisfaction.

2. Took the job expecting one thing to happen but found circumstances to be different.

3. Worked in the job during better times and can make first-hand comparisons between their current work life and the previous one. "Better times" are often perceived to be when the workload seemed easier, more work was shared, or (for long-time employees) when the company "guaranteed" employment and raises and benefits were based on criteria other than productivity.

4. Work at the job because of a money-oriented, nonwork circumstance, such as a spouse with a lower income, children in college, a bad spending habit, or large debts.

5. Had a series of negative work experiences and now can only view a job as a necessary evil.

Take a Moment

Based on the reasons for negative behavior just listed, identify complaints you've heard from Skunks in your office. Circle the number of the reason that best represents your perception of the basic complaint. (Note: It's okay to guess, because it will still provide insight.)

Point of the complaint: Reason:

_____   1 2 3 4 5

_____   Other: _____

_____   1 2 3 4 5

_____   Other: _____

_____   1 2 3 4 5

_____   Other: _____

Using the Happiness Meter

If Skunks are afoot in your company, circumstances like those mentioned mean you'll probably be sprayed with bad news. You know yourself that you're likely to tell more people about something bad than you are to share positive comments. The constant experience of customer-service departments shows that few clients call to compliment or express their satisfaction with a product or service, but those calling with complaints practically burn up the telephone wires. If we allow negative thinking, feeling, and behavior to go overboard, like Ted's, productive behavior can become typically negative Skunk behavior.

7

■ Example: Look what could happen during an employee's first week if we could mathematically calculate her happiness level:

Happiness Meter	
100%	**Day One** Marissa starts new job, eager to meet new people and make a difference.
96%	**Day Two** Marissa goes to lunch with Sue, who says she hasn't had a raise in three years and not to expect much out of the boss's promises.
94%	**Day Three** Sue's friend Brenda, who works in shipping, tells Marissa and Sue that both her department and the sales department are in disarray. People are disgruntled, and layoffs may occur.
91%	**Day Four** Sue has free time and spends it in Marissa's area, relating tales of people who have been fired and the layoffs of two years ago.
89%	**Day Five** Marissa tells Sue she ought to feel better about the company, that things aren't as bad as they seem. Sue jokingly (but with an edge of meanness, Marissa feels) tells Marissa she must be management material because she's buying into "management's lies."

Once it's on a roll, Skunk-like negativity may not let up without intervention.

Typically, after such a sequence of negative events, Marissa would experience a stabilizing period. She can do that by avoiding negative thinkers, regaining her initial enthusiasm for her job, achieving some job-related successes, and receiving praise and/or rewards from the supervisor and her organization. But once it's on a roll, Skunk-like negativity may not let up without intervention. The U.S. stock market is a perfect example. At the slightest whiff of seemingly bad news, stock prices tend to deflate. People can easily deflate, too, and what's worse, continual doses of negative input create ongoing attitude damage.

If Marissa can remain positive and strong in the face of formidable challenges at work, she won't end up with a Skunky smell. But if she's not prepared, she and others may succumb to many Skunk-like thoughts and behaviors. Even if you decide, "I'm not going to be negative," how will you maintain your positive attitude in challenging times?

Take a Moment

Examine a time in your life when a spiral of negative events caused you to feel less optimistic and to start complaining more. Try to quantify your mood level. (The events don't have to be one day apart. Just put them in chronological order and rate them.)

_____

Occurrence   Happiness level

_____

_____   _____%

_____

_____   _____%

_____

_____   _____%

Now, identify three methods you've used in challenging times to maintain a positive attitude:

_____

_____

_____

7

Keeping Things in Perspective

■ Ellen is typical of Skunks who have a tough time gaining perspective on the events of life, those people who have trouble seeing the good with the bad. At her company, she's survived two layoffs. The first one was massive and industry-wide, an attempt to stem a tidal wave of problems. At that time, Ellen's reaction was:

Ellen's Skunk-like comment:	She could have thought:
"They're just trying to get more work out of fewer people."	"Maybe some people were not producing as they should. How can I make sure I do?"
"This whole industry is going to collapse."	"This industry is facing a challenge, but perhaps the worst is now past."

■ The second round of layoffs in Ellen's industry involved far fewer people. Not the result of industry setbacks, the additional changes reflected the efforts of new management to weed out unproductive people and keep the organization competitive. Ellen was lucky, because although her negative attitude was noted with concern by management, her productivity helped her avoid a pink slip. Her comments this time:

Ellen's Skunk-like comment:	She could have thought:
"The new owner doesn't understand us or care about us. He's just out to make money."	"Maybe this owner understands business better and wants to help our organization survive."
"I was lucky the first couple of layoffs, but next time I won't be so lucky."	"With our new structure, maybe more growth and profit will be possible."

Keeping your own perspective intact, especially in the face of difficult people, challenging times, or other negative events, is possible, especially if you remember that the lives of everyone on the planet have periods of ups and downs. While we may continually seek to better ourselves or our possessions, if we always compare ourselves to extremely good or extremely bad people or circumstances, we can easily be covered with negative

Skunky smells. Remembering that comparisons are not always useful, we can tell ourselves instead that:

◆ "Things will get better."

◆ "Tomorrow is another day."

◆ "There's no real need to be negative."

But beware. Skunks won't accept such comments as encouragement to change their thinking or behavior. Remember, Skunks don't see themselves as *negative*. They see themselves as *realistic*.

> **Skunks don't see themselves as *negative*. They see themselves as *realistic*.**

Take a Moment

When making these comments to Skunks, what response did you receive?

Remark you made	Response you heard
"Oh, things will get better."	_____
	_____
"Tomorrow is another day."	_____
	_____
"Don't be so negative."	_____
	_____

7

Recognizing Skunk Behavior

Finding positive qualities in people who constantly complain can be a tough assignment for even the most optimistic of people. But like all other workplace animals, Skunks can have their good points too. If you recognize that much of their negative behavior covers up insecurities and previous hurtful experiences, you'll have a better time handling their smell.

Skunks don't like change and can seem inflexible.

For those who have difficulty accepting and dealing with change, any action can feel like a negative turn of events. Even if Skunks weren't hit by companywide layoffs, for example, their insecurities and unwillingness to change in such circumstances can make them seem inflexible and can generate additional ripples of discontent.

Skunks harbor extensive regrets over the past.

Less able than others to view all life experiences as learning opportunities, Skunks find it difficult to think, "That must have happened for a good reason, even if I don't understand it right now." Whether Skunks have had many negative experiences or only a few, they dwell on each one and see them as justification for their negative attitudes.

Skunks have been disappointed by others and focus on these losses.

Most of us take disappointments in stride and learn not to dwell on trying times, but Skunks hang on to upsetting experiences and judge everything new by them.

Just about everyone has been disappointed at one time or another. Most of us take such events in stride and learn not to dwell on trying times, but Skunks hang on to upsetting experiences and judge everything new by them. They'll remark that the new boss "acts nice, but we'll see . . ." Or they may seem paranoid when commenting that a new worker "is out to get me. I'm not sure why, but I just know . . ." Skunks find it more difficult to reestablish a sense of trust.

Because Skunks expect negative results, they act in ways that can produce them.

If you expect the worst, you often get it. A typical cycle for a Skunk is: dislike the boss ➜ resist work assignments ➜ get reprimanded ➜ spread negative comments about the boss ➜ get fired. "See?" sniffs the Skunk, "I knew it would happen all along."

Even if Skunks aren't fired in such cases, their negative influence can destroy the morale of others. That's why so many management books discuss how to fire chronically negative people.

Skunks are reactive, not proactive.

If they were proactive, they would be more positive. Proactive people see a challenge and say, "Now what can I do?" Reactive people see a challenge and fear it, thinking, "I'll wait to see what happens." If they must respond, they often respond defensively. Because they delay, Skunks may be reprimanded more than once. When the penalty eventually becomes severe, such as a warning about being fired, the Skunk says, "But I was only trying to do my job!" or, "But this happened because . . . ," placing blame on someone or something else.

Skunks needs allies.

Negative attitudes are infectious. Unlike antisocial Vipers, who need people only as an audience, Skunks need to recruit others into their armies. Skunks can be good communicators—in a twisted sort of way. By spreading negative attitudes, Skunks receive reassurance that their view is right and at the same time they let off steam—their own bottled-up energy caused by feeling negative. If you listen and support them, you'll be easily drawn into their downward spiral.

By spreading negative attitudes, Skunks receive reassurance that their view is right.

Dealing Successfully with Skunks

Following are 12 strategies for success with Skunk behavior.

Strategy 1: Keep Skunks off-balance by changing your own behavior.

7

You aren't trying knock them off their feet; you simply need to alter your strategies until you learn what works best. If you've been silent toward Skunks in the past, become more verbal. If you've been verbal, become more silent. If you supervise Skunks and keep them out of team projects, begin to include them—or conversely, if that applies. Just do something different—and keep changing. While this strategy alone won't help with the Skunk's attitude problems, it will eventually help you find strategies you can use successfully.

Strategy 2: Gently insist that good outcomes will occur.

Skunks are notorious doubters, so when you retort, "But that's not true!" or "It won't happen that way," Skunks instinctively react with resistance. Repeated gentle remarks that move the focus from all bad to not so bad or improving can help Skunks recognize that their negative words may be too harsh.

Strategy 3: Don't act *overly* positive.

Skunks put up the greatest resistance to highly positive people.

Skunks put up the greatest resistance to highly positive people. Take care to measure your positive expressions, but if you are truly positive, by all means, don't become less so just to suit Skunks! But keep in mind that Skunks don't respond well to Suzie Sunshines. When you're alone with Skunks, temper your positive comments, which only grate on their nerves and make them more aggressive. Save your energy; they can't hear you anyway.

Strategy 4: Be more assertive to combat strongly negative attitudes.

One reason Skunks succeed at infecting others with negative attitudes is because negative words travel far. Especially if you supervise Skunks, rein in their negative campaign. State explicitly that negative statements are a drain on productivity and are not appropriate in the office. If your coworker is a Skunk, refuse to repeat negative statements.

Strategy 5: Initiate change gradually.

In today's workplace, change occurs so rapidly that trying to make it gradual may seem impossible. But perhaps you can slow down or alter the change process in some way to help accommodate Skunks. Because Skunks don't deal well with change, consider how you communicate change to them and begin sharing the new information as early in the process as it becomes available. By avoiding rapid change, you help Skunks—and everyone—better avoid negative feelings and excessive stress.

Strategy 6: Demonstrate a positive outcome in an indirect but sound way.

As you respond to Skunk behavior, provide positive statements in small doses. Skunks see only the down side, not the up side, so your comments can help Skunks assemble a more complete picture.

■ **Example—**
Skunk:
Management doesn't know what they're doing! Remember a couple of years ago, when they laid off 300 people? They've hired back 300 people by now. Looks like they made a mistake.

You:
They had to lay them off then to save the company as a whole. At least they've tried to hire the same people back, and where they couldn't, new jobs were created.

Skunk:
Yeah, but all that took two years. If they'd known what they were doing in the first place, they wouldn't have had the layoff at all!

You:
It did take two years to create those 300 jobs again, but they expected it to take five. Really, management reached their goal early.

> **As you respond to Skunk behavior, provide positive statements in small doses.**

7

Strategy 7: Give Skunks the chance to create their own successes, then offer reinforcement.

Although Skunks usually gripe about *them*—the boss, their coworkers, the company—Skunks can be negative about their own achievements too. If you're working with Skunk peers or if you supervise Skunks, give them small projects or responsibilities that are easy to complete successfully (but not so easy that they're insulting). When Skunks succeed, gently reinforce the positive outcome. Then, if it's appropriate, gradually offer larger responsibilities. Remember that Skunks don't handle change well, so don't move them before they're ready. Just carve the stepping stones to success one at a time.

Strategy 8: Keep Skunks' negative aromas from wafting through the workplace.

Do what you must to limit the spread of negative news. Whether you supervise or work with Skunks, one of the best strategies is to speak with them alone, quietly explaining that their negative words are detrimental to everyone. Be as friendly as possible and offer your help. The key is to make your comments in private, not in front of others. Don't attack head to head or attempt to demoralize Skunks.

After your comments, Skunks may act rebuffed, but just let them think for a few days about what you've said. They may begin to monitor the bad words flowing from their mouths to others' ears. Or they may ask you for specific examples. When working for Skunk supervisors, your best strategy is to remain focused on your work, retain your own positive beliefs, and stand out in your company as a future-oriented thinker who can produce.

Strategy 9: Look for the real problem and help if possible.

Listen for the underlying issue behind Skunk complaints.

Instead of listening to Skunks and idly thinking, "Oh, they're so negative," listen for the underlying issue behind the complaint. Workers who always gripe about management might wish they had a promotion or more money. Those who complain that "things will never change around here" might be experiencing boredom on the job and at home. A consistent theme often emerges from the negative words, which allows you to recognize Skunks' real issues. If you have an opportunity to help improve their situations, do so.

Strategy 10: Ask for input and solutions. Give Skunks responsibility for solving problems.

Because they haven't been required to support their negative position with facts, Skunks may simply declare situations bad and then hold negative attitudes about them. Asking for their input gets Skunks involved in devising solutions and keeps their nightmare-inventing minds busy. As a supervisor, don't cancel projects just because Skunks respond, "But I said it wouldn't work!" Instead say, "I realize you feel that way. However, I know you can help us find another option."

Strategy 11: Occasionally ask Skunks to identify the worst that could happen.

When asked to speculate, Skunks' negative observations and worst-case scenarios may begin to sound extreme, even to them. But don't attempt this technique if your intention is to change behavior and prove the Skunks wrong. People change their behavior only when they're ready and only for their own reasons, not for yours.

Strategy 12: Use Skunks' negative approach to examine all sides of an issue—just don't tell them that's their purpose on the project.

Most organizations haven't thought of it, but if you put Skunks on a team project requiring review from all angles, they will find all the negative outcomes that may have been overlooked. Put this information to good use by eliminating the kind of potential problems your Skunks identified. It won't be helpful, though, if you let the Skunks, or anybody else, know their real role on the team.

If you put Skunks on a team project requiring review from all angles, they will find all the negative outcomes that may have been overlooked.

7

Take a Moment

Now that you know several strategies for success when dealing with Skunks, identify one Skunk-like coworker and two strategies you can employ to improve your interactions.

Skunk Coworker   Success Strategy

_____   _____

                                  _____

                                  Success Strategy

                                  _____

                                  _____

Next, identify a Skunk boss or subordinate and two strategies you can use to improve your interactions.

Skunk Boss or Subordinate   Success Strategy

_____   _____

                             _____

                             Success Strategy

                             _____

                             _____

Self-Check: Chapter Seven Review

Answers to these questions appear on page 99.

1. True or False?
   Skunks are not just complainers. They also like to spread negativity.

2. True or False?
   These comments work well with Skunks:
   "Things will get better."
   "Tomorrow is another day."
   "Don't be so negative."

3. Skunks don't see themselves as negative. They see themselves

   as _____.

4. Check the strategy that WILL NOT work when dealing with Skunks:

   _____ Act very positive at all times.

   _____ Be more assertive to combat strongly negative attitudes.

   _____ Initiate change gradually.

7

Chapter *Eight*

Self-Taming: How to Win Within

Chapter Objectives

▶ Check your own difficult behaviors and their possible sources.

▶ Examine how your communication style may contribute to others' difficult behaviors.

▶ Recognize the need for balance between your personal life and work life.

▶ Recognize that you are responsible for your own successes.

Case Study

Sue sat down at her desk and rested her head in her hands. She couldn't believe she'd said such negative things to Marissa, the new employee. She hadn't meant to be that critical of the company, but it seemed that once she got started, she just couldn't stop. Why had she said those things? She actually liked working here, and she certainly didn't want to start looking for another job.

"If only they'd just give me a little raise—something to show that they appreciated all of the extra work I've put in for the past three years," Sue said to herself. But when she thought about it, she could see management's side of the issue too. Things were tight across their industry, and giving raises to some employees might mean having to lay off others.

"I'll have to keep that in mind next time I feel like complaining," Sue decided.

Though you may not want to hear it, you are part of the problem. As you know by now, the behavior of every workplace animal has both good and bad qualities. Each of us sometimes exhibits difficult behaviors, even if we don't demonstrate them to the extent that you've read about in this book.

Checkpoint Questions

Although you've begun to learn better behaviors and better responses to difficult behaviors as you've worked your way through this book, now it's time to take stock of yourself and see what more you can improve. Each time you enhance your skills, you and your organization benefit. Ask yourself the following questions:

Question 1: Which types of difficult behaviors do I sometimes exhibit?

Because you're reading this book, you're searching for answers and are not likely to fall neatly into a single category. But you'll probably recognize a few difficult behaviors that hit close to home. Thoroughly review the appropriate chapters, keeping yourself in mind. Identify ways you can improve.

You'll probably recognize a few difficult behaviors that hit close to home.

Question 2: How does the atmosphere of my workplace contribute to difficult behaviors?

A dictatorship can feed all sorts of bad behaviors. Although most modern workplaces have become more democratic and there are fewer autocratic bosses, they do still exist. If your workplace has the kinds of problems identified below, perhaps your energy will be better spent in locating a new job. Ask yourself if any of these things happen:

◆ Workers are pitted against one another in a ferocious way for attention, promotions, or other rewards.

◆ The threat of termination always hangs over everyone's head.

8

◆ A disproportionate amount of physical and mental health problems exist. This can occur especially when a dictatorial boss takes over. Tragic results, such as more heart attacks, suicides, and mental breakdowns, can happen more frequently.

◆ Staff members consistently work too many hours. While not unusual during growth phases or before new people are hired, difficult behaviors are spawned when an underlying company attitude insists that everyone work "darned hard all the time."

◆ Rewards offered for performance are not given at the time of accomplishment. Dictators enjoy making the road slippery for workers, keeping them off balance.

Question 3: Does my home life or free time strongly affect my job?

Although we tend to think everyone should leave personal problems at home, it's not possible to separate ourselves into distinct compartments. Work affects our home lives in many ways, and people cannot completely ignore their feelings about home situations while they're at work.

Because your level of personal happiness affects your work, if issues in your private life are in disarray, seek counseling and take time to return some balance to your world so you can improve your overall sense of well-being. Everyone will benefit.

Question 4: Can I let my work go?

Workaholics don't make truly good employees because they have no balance in their lives. If you're working at a dead run all the time, the mind doesn't get the rest it needs to bring fresh perspective to all parts of your life. When you set a project aside for a time, your subconscious mind works on it and helps you find solutions. Answers can come in dreams . . . or when we're looking idly at a flower garden . . . or taking a shower. You've probably faced a time when you couldn't find a solution to a situation, took a break, and then the answer came to you.

When you set a project aside for a time, your subconscious mind works on it and helps you find solutions.

Balanced people are better workers because they better appreciate the value of the world and of people—two components of everyone's daily work. At the end of each day, leave your job completely behind. Enjoy the things in life you're working for. Then you can return to your workplace refreshed and with renewed perspective.

Question 5: Do I need to control or compare other people, or can I let them be themselves?

Trying to control other people takes extraordinary amounts of energy. Comparing people can make everyone look less than satisfactory and lead to judgmental thinking. Remember that people are always in the process of learning and growing. We all must make our own mistakes.

You don't have to tolerate bad attitudes and nonperformance, but it's unwise to try to force someone onto a particular path. Are the new kids just out of college too ambitious, or is their enthusiasm just what your company needs? Do the 60-year-old workers seem to rest more frequently, leaving younger employees to do "all the work," or are they acting as helpful mentors? Your perceptions may be accurate—or they may reflect your biases about age. Review your need to control or compare other people and eliminate unproductive attitudes.

Question 6: Can you truly separate people from their behavior?

Test yourself by observing your reaction to a person you know who has changed. For example, if someone has overcome the habit of dropping by your office to talk and frequently interrupting you, do you still shudder when you hear his voice in the hall? Do you still avoid him, thinking that he hasn't really changed, or can you recognize the change in behavior and offer encouragement?

8

You Are Responsible for Your Own Success

Recognize the truth of the following statements and repeat them often to yourself: *Difficult people do not control my life. I am responsible for my own success.*

If you're ready to take responsibility for your work and your life, recognize the truth of the following statements and repeat them often to yourself: *Difficult people do not control my life. I am responsible for my own success.*

Replace any negative thoughts with the knowledge that, although you may encounter people whose behavior is difficult for you to appreciate, you are handling your life. Difficulties are just hurdles you can jump—and are jumping. By applying the strategies you've learned in this book, you can help your life work better. You can move forward productively in your job and insure your own bright future.

Self-Check: Chapter Eight Review

Answers to these questions appear on page 99.

1. Which types of difficult behavior mentioned in this book best describe you, even if you don't typically exhibit difficult behaviors?

2. True or False?
   Your personal communication style may be different than your typical behavior.

3. Which of the following workplace characteristics breed difficult behaviors? Check all that apply.

   _____ Workers are pitted against one another in a ferocious way for attention, promotions, or other rewards.

   _____ An atmosphere of employee termination always hangs over everyone's head.

   _____ A disproportionate amount of physical and mental health problems exist.

8

Posttest

Answers to posttest appear on page 100.

1. When dealing with difficult personality types, the most important thing to remember is to consider that the problem is difficult _____, not difficult people.

2. Taking appropriate actions to deal with the behavior of difficult people (check one):

   _____ Will change their behavior.

   _____ Will not change their behavior.

   _____ Will not necessarily change their behavior.

3. List some successful strategies you can employ to deal with Peacock behaviors:

   _____

   _____

   _____

   _____

   _____

4. List some successful strategies you can employ to deal with Snail behaviors:

   _____

   _____

   _____

   _____

   _____

5. List some successful strategies you can employ to deal with Viper behaviors:

   _____

   _____

   _____

   _____

   _____

6. List some successful strategies you can employ to deal with Tiger behaviors:

   _____

   _____

   _____

   _____

   _____

7. List some successful strategies you can employ to deal with Koala Bear behaviors:

   _____

   _____

   _____

   _____

   _____

8. List some successful strategies you can employ to deal with Skunk behaviors:

_____

_____

_____

_____

_____

Answers to Selected Exercises

Chapter One Review (page 18)

1. False—Bad experiences do not necessarily equal bad behavior.

2. True—A good person can become a "difficult person" under the right circumstances. Remember to address the behavior.

3. True

4. a. Either/Or thinking
   b. Victory vs. Defeat thinking
   c. Progress as a Direct Path thinking

Take a Moment (page 22)

1. Peacock type 1 behavior
2. Peacock type 2 behavior
3. Peacock type 2 behavior

Chapter Two Review (page 30)

1. True

2. Peacocks typically exhibit the following difficult behaviors:
   a. Talking a lot
   b. Frequently offering unwanted advice
   c. Interrupting too much
   d. Taking over when it's not their place

3. Listen MORE. Peacock egos needs it, and it will help you get useful results.

4. True

Chapter Three Review (page 42)

1. Snails do not like making decisions.

2. To get results with Snails, carefully outline the work to be done, set a <u>deadline,</u> and get Snails to <u>agree.</u>

3. True

4. True

Chapter Four Review (page 50)

1. True

2. Low

3. "You're just too sensitive."

   "Can't you take a joke?"

4. True

Chapter Five Review (page 62)

1. True

2. False

3. Workaholics

4. Assertive body language. Purposely keep eye contact. In conversation, pull back your shoulders and stand strong, even if you feel like you're losing the argument.

5. True

Chapter Six Review (page 70)

1. True—Koala Bears need a high degree of people contact.

2. Time

3. True—Mistakes are part of the learning process.

4. True

Chapter Seven Review (page 87)

1. True

2. False—These responses DO NOT work with Skunks.

3. Skunks don't see themselves as negative. They see themselves as <u>realistic.</u>

4. The WRONG action to take with a Skunk is to act very positive at all times. Skunks typically respond to a high level of positiveness with skepticism, suspicion, and/or jealousy. It's better to be more assertive to combat strongly negative attitudes and initiate changes gradually.

Chapter Eight Review (page 93)

1. Answers will vary.

2. True

3. All three answers listed indicate an unhealthy workplace.

Posttest

1. Behavior

2. Taking appropriate actions to deal with the behavior of difficult people will not necessarily change their behavior.

3.–8. Answers will vary—see appropriate chapters for successful strategies.